All Scripture references taken from the KJV

of the Bible, unless otherwise indicated.

Fantasy Spirit Spouse

by Dr. Marlene Miles

ISBN: 978-1-960150-19-6

Paperback Version

Table of Contents

Fantasy Spirit Spouse

Freshwater Press

USA

What?

What in the world is a *spirit spouse*?

There are at least 30 different types of *spirit spouses*. This book will primarily talk about one type, and it will be discussed as it pertains to *soul prosperity*. From the first 3 books in this series, **The Motherboard: Key to Soul Prosperity**, **Souls in Captivity**, and **Soul Prosperity: Your Health & Your Money** we have learned that memory is an integral part of the soul's prosperity. The mind and its internal workings are important, and it wields power both in the Earth and in the spirit. The mind is one of the three parts of the soul. As a review, the other two components of the soul are the emotions and the will.

The soul should not be played with as it is powerful and can be dangerous to the user and others if it is misused. Most of the books in this series are about the emotions and how the emotions can affect each of our lives.

I write a list and a brief synopsis of the types of spirit spouses for your reference, and you may want to study this out for yourself. To date, I am not an expert on all of these, but I do know something of *Fantasy Spirit Spouse* as the Lord has taught me what I am sharing with you. if the Lord shares more with me I will convey it to you either in a book or in a video message on my YouTube channel. Spirit spouse is a huge and vast subject, and I will be attentive if the Lord imparts more to me.

Fantasy Spirit Spouse

Dearly beloved, I beseech *you* as strangers and pilgrims, ***abstain from fleshly lusts, which war against the soul;***
Having your conversation honest among the Gentiles that, whereas they speak against you as evildoers, they may by your good works which they shall behold, glorify God in the day of visitation.
1 Peter 2:11-12 *(emphasis added, mine)*

I will mention here and cannot overstress to be careful with *fantasy* which we as children call *imagination*. As kids, we are taught that it is okay or even encouraged to use our imaginations, but too much imagination or the wrong kind of imagination can be *very dangerous* when taken too far as children, but even more so as adults.

Imagination or fantasy can be extremely dangerous when added to grown up activities, namely, **sex**.

Working together with the *spirit of lust*, imagination when tied to sex can invoke or conjure up things that are more than fleeting, more than fantasy, more than simple imagination. *Lust* works against soul prosperity. A person oppressed or possessed by this *spirit* will not prosper in their soul.

Many things in our world are temporary and throw-away, but if we conjure up something from the pit of hell or something from the pit of hell may use what you've imagined and take license to tag along or link up with what you've imagined, and this may not be temporary at all. This is how evil fantasies come into people's lives. Further, what is conjured up or visiting from *hell* may not go back there – easily--, or ever.

Humans, using their powerful minds and imaginations can summon up things that **do not go away.** When man is using his mind to create something he wants he calls it *manifesting.* When he is using his mind but creates or draws something to himself that he doesn't want, it's still manifesting, but he has no control over what has come to him. Moreso, it depends on your spiritual state--, are you saved? Yes? Are you walking upright before the Lord? Then you have a guardian angel who assists in your "manifesting."

If you are saved but carnal, saved and still sinning or unsaved you may have been assigned a guardian demon. That demon, a fallen angel will then be your manifesting assistant. Can you guess what you'll get using your powerful imagination then?

Your imagination is the same and it is still powerful whether you use it for good or for evil, if the Lord allows. Careful.

Let's say you broke up with your spouse or significant other. You can't get him or her off of your mind. You want them back. You can't have them back for whatever reason but because you think of them 24/7, because of your mind and your powerful memory a soul tie is created. Let's say you IMAGINE that they are back with you and that's how you fall asleep every night, reminiscing, remembering the good times, and that keeps the soul tie going strong.

Let's say you saw or met the object of your desire, but you never had a chance to date them. You only IMAGINE that the two of you are together because you read online or in a book that is how you *"create"* your future, that is how you *"create"* what you want. You've been doing that for days, nights, weeks, months, years. That has also created a fantasy soul tie.

Let's say you have no one but you visit porn sites, and you *imagine* that you are one of the parties in the sex acts that you are viewing online. You have formed a soul tie with the porn actors. I kid you not. You have formed a fantasy soul tie, and this can cause of a lot of trouble. Especially when and because sex is involved.

What kind of sex?

Any **kind of illegal sex.**

What kind of sex is illegal? Do you mean perverse or freaky sex?

Illegal sex is **any** and every kind, type, or act of sex that you have with anyone who is NOT your legally married spouse. Even if you are just watching it. Even if you are watching it online, on TV or at the theatre. Even if you're fantasizing while *with* your spouse. ***What?***

But It's Just Me

But what if you're not watching
anything – **it's just you?**

Even when it's *just* **<u>you</u>** maybe even
especially when it's just you and your
imagination is going wild.

There are more than 30 different kinds
of *spirit spouses*, one type is the *Fantasy Spirit
Spouse*. That type comes from what you *thunk*
up in your own mind. Either fantasizing that
you are still together with someone you desire
who is gone from your life (for whatever
reason), or you have your own make-believe
whatever that allows you to **imagine** you have
a "person," a "friend," or a marriage partner.
This *"person"* may be totally in your

imagination, or they may be what you imagine when you take out the lotions, and oils, and/or the ***devices***.

It could be conjured up by what you look at on the hidden videos that no one knows you have. No matter how you got to those videos–, whether you searched directly, typing them into your computer's search bar, or something scandalous popped up on your screen, so you claim innocence because you didn't *search* for it directly. You didn't type it in, but you watch it anyway.

Demons could be invited or called up when you watch, repeatedly or even one time any of those movies that you knew or even didn't know were filled with racy scenes of sex and nudity. There is no reason to spy out another's liberty, especially since the Word of God tells us not to do that. It brings man into bondage.

And that because of false brethren unawares brought in, who came in privily to spy out our liberty which we have in Christ Jesus, that they might bring us into bondage: Galatians 2:4

The *fantasy spirit spouse* could have come by the "relaxation" devices that you use, that are hidden in some odd place in your home, that you think no one knows you have.

This may be a long explanation as to why your momma told you not to do some of the things that she told you not to do when you were a child, but she didn't tell you why.

I'm telling you why.

You're welcome.

A Demon by Any Other Name

A demon by any other name is still a demon.

Prayerlessness and carelessness leave the **saved** or unsaved open to spirit spouse attack. Other names of spirit spouse are, husband of the night, wife of the night, nightmares, dream husband, dream wife, incubus, succubus, Lilith.

Here's the list with brief descriptions that was promised:

Marine spirit spouse-- the majority of spirit spouses are from the evil water (marine kingdom). They look beautiful. Think of mermaids, mermen, or merfolk when thinking of these entities.

Resident spirit spouses are disembodied beings, they believe that humans are their 'homes" or house. They usually squat there while people are sleeping or dreaming. However, in the presence of God it is too hot for them. So stay prayed up.

Giant spirit spouses are spiritual devil prostitutes. They are remnants from Genesis 6:6.

Serpentine spirit – snake spirit spouses. May appear as ½ human and ½ fish or ½ snake. Can look beautiful as queens or kings with crowns on their heads.

Ancestral spirit spouses. Pose as living or dead ancestors to the victim. They can be *familiar* and *monitoring spirits* and will sleep with any- or everyone in a family.

Physical spirit spouse- when a spirit spouse manifests as a physical human being. If you see someone who is too good looking to be true, beware. They can appear and disappear at will—even right before your eyes. You're not crazy – that really happened.

***Projected spirit spouse*-** witch doctors, voodoo priests, occultists, etc. can use astral projection to have spiritual sex with a victim. (Eccl 12:6)

Fantasy or ***Imagination spirit wife/husband***. Your mind, your imagination is the drawing board of your destiny, according to Minister Geoff Uzo. Usually, there is no memory or the sexual event in the victim; it has been wiped away, but there may be physical evidence that sex actually happened.

Bloodline spirit spouses (lust, polygamy spirit spouses)– (genetic spirit spouses). Transferred from consensual sex before conception. **PRAY before you have relations with your own spouse.**

Idol spirit – a person attracts generational curses when they worship idol *gods* and end up being married to these idol gods. For example all shamans have spirit spouses. They want them and believe that it helps them in their powers.

Dwarf spirit husband/wife- some women think these demons are their future children because of their size, but this is not so.

Disembodied spirit spouses are demons with no spiritual bodies. They define themselves in deliverance as, *"Nobody."*

Strongman spiritual spouse of generational and family curses. They sponsor other demons and control them. They call themselves the boss, the mighty, terrible, landlord, the leader. They store up people's blessings over the years in a spiritual strong room.

Leviathan spirit spouses are the old-world serpent in charge of water snakes, mermaids, mermen, and merfolk. Harder to dislodge. Need a seer who is prophetic and apostolic to get deliverance. Works with Asmodee (Asmodeus), a wicked sexual demon whose goal is to defile humans.

Animal spirit spouses. Animals are not meant to be seen in the dream. You have got to stay prayed up. Pray a wall of fire, a hedge of fire, a mountain of fire around you before sleep.

Strange man or strange woman spirit spouses physically attack natural spouses. The have and use powers such as telekinesis. These are the kind that horror movies are made of. They fly around and can move things around in the house—right before your very eyes.

Old man or old woman spirit spouses usually torment people of younger age with sex in the dream. Things rattle around, causing noises in the house and even pictures can fall off the wall. They make a young person look old, and then no none wants to marry them because their beauty is gone.

Transferred spirit spouses can come from working in deliverance and ministry, et cetera. Any possession, object or person can *transfer* spirits. To guard against this, DO NOT SHARE personal items with people--, nobody, not a best friend, not even a family member. Period.

Territorial spirit spouses. Every river, house, enclave or subdivision has ruling or territorial demons over those areas. They have legal right or authority to be there. Just because you can't see them, doesn't mean that they are not there and operating. They think they own everything including people in "their" area/territory.

Hermaphrodite spirit spouses show up as transgendered by whatever means that will work for the evil they plan to inflict on the victim. They can turn a woman into a man or turn a man into a woman and they become the gender required to attack them. They are vicious and violent.

Hidden spirit spouses don't even show up in the dream. They are not interested in sex in the dream. But they cause disease, tragedies, and block successes and breakthroughs.

Masquerading spirit spouses is the typical identity theft. They are crafty and tricky. They use the face of familiar people so that they will be accepted while you let down your guard and may consent to dream sex. Works with the *spirit of lust.* If you are the lusting type and someone, anyone presents to you with dream sex, you'll probably agree to it.

Multiple spirit spouses – when a person experiences more than one sexual partner during the dream. Gang stalkers. Gang rape. Group sex, orgy type sex in the dream.

Incestuous spirit spouses happen in magic, New Age, witchcraft type of homes. Some parents marry their own children to their "spirit guides" for power or for protection or rites of passage. It is all demonic.

Witchcraft or warlock spirit spouses when you consult a witchdoctor you get initiated whether you know it or not. You become a **blind witch** that means you are a witch and do not even know it. Period. A spirit spouse is assigned as soon as you visit anyone practicing in the dark arts.

Celebrity spirit spouses speaks for itself. Memorabilia has familiar spirits attached to them. It's all a masquerade though.

Transference spirit spouses—pastors, doctors, intercessors, et cetera should be mightily prayed up so this doesn't happen. Countertransference is possible also when the deliverance worker, pastor, doctor, massage therapist, et cetera transfers *their* demons to their clients/customers/patients. Best to stay prayed up and consider who you are putting your hands on and who is putting their hands on you. Sometimes touch is not even involved, some transference can happen just be being in association with a person in in their vicinity.

Manifested spirit spouses show up first in the dream, but later they take a human form and show up in the natural.

Graveyard spirit spouse or necromancer spirit spouses attach to a person from visiting cemeteries, graveyards, going to funerals, et cetera. Demons can follow folks home. Sometimes called stubborn pursuers. I've never once heard a person officiating a funeral pray for anything more than peace, comfort and strength to the family of the deceased. I've heard NO ONE ever pray for the general protection of the attendees at the memorial, wake, funeral or interment.

Desert spirit spouses can attach to people who are not prayed up but go to certain areas where demons have been displaced to.

Forest spirit spouses-, it depends on what kind of forest it is – if it's a dedicated forest or a dedicated grove, hikers, hunters, et cetera beware. These demons can follow people home, stalk them and become dream sex partners.

(This list comprised from Minister Geoff Uzo)

Grossed out yet? You should be.

Sex demons entrap, enslave, capture and ruin lives, destiny and the destiny of entire bloodlines.

It's Only Entertainment

Oh, you're probably thinking I'm taking this too far. I'm not. Any person who this has happened to and has struggled for months and possibly years to break free of the torment and the attacks will tell you that I'm not.

Porn, for example, is not just entertainment. It may be make believe because that kind of stuff, those kinds of plot lines (if you call them plots) don't happen in the real life, but it does happen in evil spiritual realms where the devil and his demons are thinking up the most perverse things, they can so they can defile man, transfer demons to him, and then go an accuse him to God. Further this stuff can happen with lusty and demonized people. So if you roll up on someone who is hot to trot and *ready to go* at a moment's notice with a complete stranger, and you're the complete stranger, don't let that go to your head; they are demonized or drugged up out of their head, or both.

The pit of hell is where most of these demonic producers, directors and even actors are pulling this stuff from. All pornography is demonic and the producers, directors and actors are almost exclusively satanists or will become satanists.

In a world where the word, *"Christian"* is put in front of anything, *Christian* jazz, *Christian* rap, *Christian whatever*, there is no such thing as Christian porn, because porn is from hell.

Whatever you conjure up or watch with regularity, especially when **sex** is tied to it, ties you to that thing. A soul tie doesn't have to tie you to something bad, it is just that soul ties are not good because a tied soul cannot prosper, especially when it is tied to something from hell a demon calling itself *spirit spouse*.

It--, this sex demon, this *spirit spouse* may even appear in your dreams in a masquerade as the image that you fantasize about or watched on the movie. It will appear in the image that *"does it for you." **That*** is not a mystery handsome man or gorgeous woman that you may or may not have seen before either in person, or online or on TV; that is a demon masquerading as something that you *think* is attractive.

That is not a dirty little secret. It is neither little, nor is it a secret, except maybe to you and some other humans – *right now.* That is a demon. It has been conjured up by you, by a sex spell and you are the witch or the wizard who conjured it up. Blindly. Possibly. But, when a person casts spells even unknowingly, they are still doing witchcraft and they are a blind witch. **<u>Repent</u>**. This is not playtime.

Sex Magic

But the cowardly, the unbelieving, the vile, the murderers, the sexually immoral, **those who practice magic arts**, the idolaters and all liars—they will be consigned to the fiery lake of burning sulfur. This is the second death.

Revelations 21:8

In the natural, this illegal sex with *just* you, or you and another, or *others* includes not just the people you see, there is at least one demon present and *involved* in the sex act with you--, a sex demon, a spirit spouse.

Here's where fantasy becomes real and it's not a good thing.

Sobering. Very sobering. Women, especially wake up with marks and scratches on their body that there is NO way they could have or would have scratched themselves like that and have stayed asleep.

Sleep paralysis is a sign of spirit spouse. Feeling the bed go down but there is no one there; there is--, it is spirit spouse. You may wake up with signs of having had sex, but you were alone and were not having sex the night before or during the night. Spirit spouse.

Spirit Spouse

This is a horror if you haven't realized that yet.

Further, once invited, once involved, once **attached** to you, *spirit spouse* is stubborn and VERY difficult to be rid of because it **thinks** it is married to you.

And there you are, a confirmed bachelor, never wanting to get married. Or you couldn't find any girl good enough. But you've chosen a *demon?* Are you serious right now? The sex you have alone is so mind blowing that no human can measure up. Actually, you should not be sampling this anyway. This is why God said in His Word, **Do not fornicate**. One reason why not is *spirit spouse*. Remember there may be more than one and they've been either studying you since birth, or earlier. They know exactly what you like, what you want. All the while you are in the throes of passion they are stealing from you, giving you diseases, taking your money and opportunities and ruining your destiny. But you won't know that until later, **unless you believe God**. If you can't hear God, then believe this book. Then just ask God if this is true.

Now the things that people say and yell during sex, they can become as *word curses, incantations and spells*. No kidding. More witchcraft, invoking sex spells. Sex spells is a real thing, and it is NOT of GOD. Illegal sex is bad enough, but if someone is telling you what words to use and what to **SAY** at certain times of the act—you should have already run out of there, but right now, RUN!

Repent.

This book has gone here, wow! It's blowing my mind too. Spirit spouse is a soul UN-prosperer. Be in health and prosper as your soul prospers? Yeah, that's of God. Spirit spouse *undoes* a lot of good in a human.

Wisdom is better than weapons of war: but
one sinner destroyeth much good.

Ecclesiastes 9:18

That sinning demon – that's what
demons do – they sin, they get you to sin and
that undoes a lot of good. Sins in general and
sex sins in particular defile you and
indoctrinates you into sin confirming your
sinship when you should have a confirmed
sonship in Christ.

Or you, young lady, *saving* yourself
until marriage. Unless you have ZERO sex
ever, you haven't *saved* anything. Worse you
may have thrown everything away especially
the people who try to redefine what sex is. The
world says it's okay to do any and all of this,
but it is NOT. Surely, while you were waiting
on Prince Charming you didn't intend to marry
a demon, did you? A frog would have been
better, but a frog is not what God has for you,
either.

Spirit Children

In Psalm 144:7-8, the Psalmist cried out to God to deliver him from evil children, calamities and out of great waters. "Out of great waters." We need deliverance from the powers of the water and their *strange children*. In order for anyone to have a child in the spirit realm, it means you are already married to a spirit spouse.

Yes, with parts and pieces of your humanity the devil creates *spirit children.*

You may have seen them already. You may have heard them, depends on your sensitivity. Those darling masquerades in your dreams of babies, cute children and the like are not God showing you what your children will look like when you have them, necessarily – although God can do whatever God wants if you are walking upright before Him.

Spirit children is not in the scope of this book, but isn't it amazing that even the devil knows that marriage comes before children.

A person could not even be aware that they have spirit spouse. The memory of the dream is completely stolen from the victim they wake up and go about life as if nothing happened. But everything happened. How many of us and for how many years? LORD help us.

A person could be somewhat aware that they have a spirit spouse. For example a married person could think they are so in love with their spouse that they dream about them at night and have sex with them even in the dream. It's a masquerade.

If you are a lusty person, you could be having sex with an in-law, a friend or a relative in the dream and feel like you're getting over. You may feel that your spouse doesn't even know. It's also a masquerade; you're having sex with a demon. Pray and ask God to show you who (what) you are really having sex with in the dream. Brace yourself.

We discussed the multiple spirit spouse, but I want to add that it is called the **polygamous spirit spouse**, same demon, different faces. This really works on the lusty person who wants "different" all the time. Sometimes men are so clever that they are actually duped!

Lord, we need deliverance!

Prayer Points:

- Lord, I repent of every evil thing I've done and imagined that has drawn spirit spouse to me in the name of Jesus.

- I renounce all soul ties created. I renounce and denounce the behavior and I break every evil covenant that has been formed because of my sin, rebellion, ignorance and stupidity in the Name of Jesus.

• Every soul tie connecting me to a spirit husband or wife, break!
• Any power masquerading as my spouse in the dream, die!
• Every wedding ring of the spirit spouse has place on my hand, in the name of Jesus, I remove it and I command it to catch fire!
• Every wedding certificate linking me to a spirit husband/wife, in the name of Jesus, catch fire! BURN! BURN! BURN!
• Anything planted into my body to seduce me by the spirit husband/wife, in the name of Jesus, catch fire!
• Holy Ghost fire arise, incubate my body with your fire in Jesus name.
• O God arise and repair any damage done to my body by any spirit spouse.
• Every wicked power using the face of a familiar person to sleep with me in my dream, die!

- *Spirit of lust,* I bind you ad cast you out in the name of Jesus.

Weird Diseases

Weird and mystery diseases may be happening to you; this is result of spirit spouse sex. Can't get rid of that yeast infection. Wonder why?

Irregular period? Bleeding too often, especially? Let me tell you why. That demon, those demons come for blood. When this oppression becomes worse – a possession, you are like a possession to these demons – a toy. It's as though something has control over your menstrual flow. Let's say something upsets you and now your menses starts, out of cycle—you just finished last week for goodness sakes. That night you may be attacked in your dream because you are on the altar of evil and the demon wants blood.

Let's say your are perimenopause or past menopause, why are you having a random menses? Spirit spouse. It wants blood.

What do they want? Many things.

Blood. Blood makes covenant. If they make 'covenant' then they feel they have a legal right to you any time they want.

They want to stop you from marrying in the natural because you may bring forth righteous seed. They want to defile you so God will turn His back on you. To thwart your ministry, destiny, life. The devil hates you. Once defiled, you repent and pray then tomorrow God gives you new mercies. Did you just miss a whole day outside of the presence of God because of being defiled? Did you have to sit outside the gate for the whole day because of being unclean?

YOU HAVE TO STAY PRAYED UP!

Sex is also the perfect way to introduce other and worse demons into your life and *into* YOU.

I hope you are realizing how much warfare there is being a human in the Earth!

You need deliverance!

While the devil hates you he wants what you are, what you have. Your soul. He will take fragments of it at a time, as we have discussed. He wants your humanity because there are special gifts, blessings, authority and POWER that God has given you, that the devil doesn't have and will never get. Recall he is a fallen angel, not a fallen human. **Fallen humans can be redeemed, fallen angels have no redemption**. He's looking at the abyss, brimstone and fire for Eternity.

In Christ we are looking at Heaven for all Eternity. But we have to study to show ourselves approved. We have to work while it is yet day. We have to work out our Salvation with fear and trembling.

Spooky Family

The saving grace in either of the above scenarios is if you realize what you've done wrong, or what an ancestor has done and repent quickly and turn immediately from that path of sin and also repent for your ancestors, ask God for Mercy and to break all the evil ancient covenants that are negatively affecting you.

If you're innocent and you've been sent a spirit spouse by some witch or wizard, that's another whole warfare.

This spirit spouse demon thinks you have a family together and it plans to stay with you all your life and into your bloodline, some say to the third and fourth generations; but I've also heard it said to the 10th and up to the 14th generations of a bloodline.

If you are into illegal sex, or if anyone in your bloodline was, you may have gotten yourself a spirit spouse, or inherited one. When your dreams are filled with marriage and spirit-spouse-related images, GOD is mercifully trying to show you what you need to pray for or against. You have to discern the source of the dreams because they could be devil-inspired dreams where the devil is showing you something he wants to do or introduce into your life, and excuse me, if you don't know that, you may swoon and think this is wonderful and ACCEPT it.

You accept it by:

1. Doing nothing. If there are no prayers to undo it or cancel it, then you essentially are accepting it.
2. Being happy about it. Not having wisdom enough to know that what you think is a blessing is a curse if devastating.
3. Thinking it's a great secret between you and God and never even

happening to tell someone who may know Bible dream interpretation. Devastating.

4. You begin telling others about it--, the wrong someone's. The more you speak it (in faith), the sooner it will come to pass.

5. And, if you're an artist, and/or prophetic you may start to draw pictures of what you saw in your dream, making it that much closer to coming to reality. This is another form of witchcraft and spellbinding.

Family Secret

Is spirit spouse something you wanted to give your kids and your grandkids of either gender? Of course not!

Spirit spouse assumes the gender you are interested in, but it is an **it** --, it's a demon.

Spirit spouses are vicious, evil, brutal, even murderous. They block you from getting married, staying married, and sometimes from having natural children of your own because they hate children. They hate boyfriends, girlfriends, fiancées, fiancés, spouses and they hate children.

This is one thing that you can't ignore. You can't ignore spirit spouse to make it go away. You can't ignore it thinking that when you go on to Glory that that thing will just die too, it won't. It will not only live on, as it has for millennia, it will transfer to your children, it may even be attacking them in their sleep now, even while you are still alive! It doesn't care!

What!

Yup.

You're watching mature audience movies. You're watching porn. Your kids are asleep, so you think the kids don't know. Maybe your kids don't know exactly what you're doing, just as you do't know exactly what your ancestors did. But the results of what you've done will show up sooner or later.

You get a spirit spouse; do you think it's going to stop with you? Some of these demons sleep with everyone in the family, *even children*. Talk about no respecter of people. If you're not prayed up and you're living a sinful lifestyle, **who is covering your kids in prayer?** Oh, you think you are? You are not in right alignment with God, so how can you be the intercessor or the covering for your children?

The pastor? He can in a limited way, but that's your job. Is his "prayer covering" stopping you from sinning? The anointing flows from the "head." You are the head of your family; your sin is stopping the anointing that could be flowing in your home and family.

One of my friends who is a marriage and family counselor says, "Sometimes parents are the worse things that can happen to a child."

Don't let that be you.

If you have either chosen or found yourself as a parent – especially if you *chose* to be a parent, you've got to teach your children, nurture your children, feed, clothe and educate them. You also have to cover them not just physically with a house and clothing but cover them spiritually because they cannot cover themselves while they are still children with their immature, unprospered little souls.

__Your__ soul should already be grown up and prospering in the things of God.

Don't Let That Ring be an Heirloom

That ring on your finger that you can feel the weight of, but there is no ring there. That is not the nostalgia of when you were married. That is not (necessarily or usually) the Lord letting you know that you will soon be married again because it's been so long since your divorce. That's not some kind of neuralgia where you need to go to the neurologist and have your left ring finger checked because you *feel* a ring on it.

You don't need to go see a shrink either; you're not crazy--, you're spiritual. Yes, you are, if you feel a ring on your left ring finger, but there is no visible ring there.

That is spirit spouse, laying a claim on you. it thinks it has married you. There may be wedding apparel, a wedding certificate and even wedding photos somewhere in the spiritual realm indicating that you two actually got married. If you saw yourself in a dream getting married, that's not (most likely not) God showing you your future; that's spirit spouse. Especially if you can't see the face of the "person" you married, you are most likely married to some demon, a spirit spouse.

You've got some praying to do to get out of this. You've got some fasting to do. You may need to find a deliverance minister/pastor, prophet, prophetess, intercessor or apostle to fire the demon(s) that believe they are married to you.

Don't start none, won't be none – it is so much easier to stay out of this kind of trouble than it is to *get* out of it.

But how will you know that you actually *have* a spirit spouse?

Following is a short list of symptoms and signs. It is not exhaustive because I don't know all the devil's tricks and I don't know what new tricks he's developed since I wrote this book. YESTERDAY.

Other Signs

Anxiety.

Asthma, especially when it develops in older people, suspect marine (water) kingdom: spirit spouse.

Bad dreams.

Children in dreams, hearing children in the house when there are no children in the house. Spirit spouse creates spirit children, which is another whole book, that unless the Lord tells me to write it, it is a book for someone else to pen.

Depression, either the emotional kind or you feel the bed goes down when there is no one there. Some people report seeing the bed go down when there is no one there.

Eerie feelings.

Foul odor. Sometimes an odor is about you that others can smell or even you can smell, but you can't seem to get rid of it. Spirit spouse.

Gnashing of teeth – (this is my personal opinion.)

Hearing noises in your house.

Ichabod. When spirit spouse is in your life, it steals your glory – your glory leaves you. Have you noticed that you used to walk in the favor of God, but that has mysteriously and suddenly changed? Spirit spouse defiles and steals virtues.

Jealousy. Spirit spouse is jealous and dangerous.

Kill. Spirit spouse will kill your destiny, your soul's prosperity, your ministry, your life, if it can. It wants you to itself so it kills relationships and may not stop there. I've read stories of fiancé's and spouses mysteriously dying right before or after the wedding. Evil, mysterious human agents may be involved--, but the perp may not always be the spouse, the boyfriend, the wife, or the girlfriend as the police often suspect.

Loneliness. Spirit spouse wants you to itself and will separate you from your own spouse friends, and even children. It will put a reproach on you and people may reject you for unknown or no real reasons.

Hold on to your job because spirit spouse also wants you broke. Just think of the worst red-neck, jealous, controlling or ghetto spouse you can, that's what spirit spouse is, or even worse.

Monitoring spirits. A sense that someone is there, yeah, watching you. Familiar spirits watch you. Makes sense doesn't it, that's what a controlling spouse would do.

Nightmares, night terrors

Over the counter meds fill your house trying to "fix" whatever is wrong with you. You're spending hundreds or thousands of dollars on things to try to fix your odd symptoms that no doctor is able to find a reason for.

Pettiness against your spouse for no real reason. Spirit spouse is whispering in your ear everything that is wrong with your spouse. It is also whispering in your spouse's ear either everything that's wrong with you or making one or both of you convinced that your spouse will suffer dire consequences or die if they don't leave you of if you don't leave your spouse. It may not be lying because if will try to effect a disaster, any disaster to get rid of your spouse if it wants you.

If you are listening to the whispers of demons, without even realizing that you are listening to you will begin to hate your covenanted spouse or boyfriend or girlfriend that you used to love so much, and not even know why. Their jokes are no longer funny. They can't do anything right, quick enough. You hate their hair, the way they eat. You hate everything about them, suddenly.

That's spirit spouse, a professional demon excelling at driving a wedge between HUMANS who are in covenant. God hates broken covenant, when you break it, when your spouse breaks it and when the two of you let a demon break it. You two should be in covenant with God in it, a three fold cord that is not easily broken. (Eccl)

Quarrels with your real spouse if you have one, and for no good reasons. Spirit spouse's assignment is to break you two up.

Rejection and reproach from real humans for no reason at all.

Seeing images of ugly things when you close your eyes. Depends on your spiritual sensitivity, though.

Torment

Uneasiness. You don't even want to go to bed. Are you like a child again?

Vicious. In addition to being jealous, spirit spouse is vicious. Depending on how deeply it is rooted into your life determines to what ends it will go to either have you all to itself or ruin your life altogether, or both.

Worry- this whole book series started out with how not to worry in the book, The Motherboard. And look where we are again.

Xenomorphic is something that is alien in appearance or form. If you have enough courage to ask the Lord to actually show you your spirit spouse, He will. When you're ready and you are likely to see anything from a horror movie to a cartoon figure, but mostly it will be a demon. Amorphic in that it may have the head of something and the body of a snake or a crocodile, an octopus. Usually it will be something from the evil water kingdom. Ask God. Really, ask Him. The reality check will help your prayer life because you will want that THING far away from you.

Yowza! Your life is hijacked.

Zenith of torment misery and manipulation.

I Recently Met One

I, myself have both met and been confronted by a spirit spouse. BTW each party in a relationship or marriage can have a spirit spouse, or even more than one spirit spouse.

We all really need God; we need spiritual protection always.

So, this confrontation--, I mentioned it in **Blindsided: Has the Old Man Bewitched You?**

I was at a friend's house whom I fancied to be a boyfriend. It was a Sunday afternoon, and he was doing *whatever* in his house moving from the kitchen to the garage and back to the kitchen again. He was working on some manly-type project. I fell asleep on his living room couch. I don't think I was asleep long, but in the dream, I saw a woman walking heavily, quickly, as she was a a road of some sort, with green trees in the background. She was barreling towards me. She was either moving so fast that she appeared as a hologram, or there were three of them. I could focus on the main one in the middle and there was a half a one on either side of her. At least that was the image I saw. If there were three of them, they all looked alike to me. She had a round face, she was kind of plump and fair complected. She was wearing a green dress, simple in style. She really didn't have a good figure, but hey, she's a spirit so what shape she assumed is her business. (It's business, these things don't have genders, they assume genders for the masquerades.) So she's stomping toward me angrily.

Now, as my style is, I decided to wake up; I do that within a dream rather often. Anyway, I woke up and I may have been a little shocked, but I knew this was a dream or some kind of vision, so I willed myself out of sleep and prayed immediately. Boyfriend was in the garage or wherever and he's not spiritual anyway, so I really didn't have anyone to talk to at that time about this.

As a matter of fact, I'm not sure why I fancied him a boyfriend. I think it was early in the relationship and I was still trying to really know who he was.

Find out as soon as you can who a person really is, who their God is and what altars they serve at. It is really a bad idea, to be unequally yoked.

Okay, so I wake up, but I remain horizontal on the couch because often when I want to recall a dream or vision I stay in the exact same position where I had the dream or vision until I can recollect all the details that I can by help of the Holy Spirit.

I'm awake, but in my "understanding" now the woman is standing at the foot of the couch speaking to me (in the spirit), "He *doesn't want you; he wants me. He's not staying here with you; he's going with me.*"

As it happens, Boyfriend was stationed in another country but on leave for some months, and it was up in the air as to whether he would go back overseas for another stent, or if he would remain stateside. I said nothing back to her, because this is non-verbal, as I said, and even though I had been to his house many times, I was not comfortable talking to what would have looked like *myself* there. The family room was adjoined to the kitchen and the kitchen was adjacent to the garage, so...

However, either to try to torment me or being braggadocious, his green-dress-wearing spirit spouse kept repeating the same thing again and then a third time. I got up from the couch and began my pacing—which means now I'm praying. I purposely walked and prayed in the area of the couch where I perceived that she stood. I no longer sensed her presence there, but I kept praying in tongues. I prayed in the Spirit for 10 or 15 minutes, firmly, but not loudly. I don't know how long and then "she" (it) was gone; things were quiet again.

I continued to pray as to how to handle this and I asked the Holy Spirit what I should do. Really, I asked, *"Should I tell him?* Knowing he's not spiritual at all, I had to ask.

The answer I got was a definite, ***"Tell him."***

I Told Him

About a half an hour later when he returned from the garage, or wherever and we sat at the kitchen island, I bluntly told him, *"You have a spirit spouse."*

I did not expect a favorable response, but since I had asked if I should tell him and I was told that I *should* tell him, it is now my responsibility to tell him. I knew this would be a turning point, but I didn't yet know in which direction. Truthfully, I didn't care in which direction this turned because now with a Word from the Lord, my focus is to be obedient to the God and all will be well with me.

He asked, *"What is that? What is a spirit spouse?"*

I told explained spirit spouse to him, more generally than in this book because I do not know what "kind" of spirit spouse it or they were, but I suspect at least one was fantasy, based on certain behaviors that I had witnessed by *Boyfriend*.

He didn't believe me (not surprised). He thought I was weird. (I expected that) and pretty much stopped speaking to me, (I also expected that). BUT! I did the will of Him who sent me. I told Boyfriend the truth that was either seed or watering and perhaps one day when he is ready, he can receive the Truth and be set free and live his own life instead of a demon living its illegal life through him, while he suffers.

Is he suffering?

Yes. His money is hit substantially, it is why he is overseas; it is for financial reasons. His relationships either suffer or they are non-existent. I think this spirit spouse, or these spirit spouses are well-rooted in his life. Boyfriend's spiritual giftings are substantial but there are so many blockages down his family line and in his own life by his own doings that without deliverance he will probably remain captive. I have threatened more than once to "go get him," but you can't go get someone against their will, it will make matters far worse for them.

Of course, Boyfriend and types like him believe they are *free*. They believe they are living life on their own terms. There is no spouse controlling them. They believe they come and go as they please, but spiritually they may not have a clue that they are on lockdown. An illegal, disembodied spirit is squatting in his house (body) living *another* life (it's had many through the ages) while Boyfriend's soul and spirit are captive and imprisoned, but he thinks he's free. What a tremendous and sad deception.

Worse, while he runs and runs, like so many men do to get away from any women that they think may want to "trap" them. Boyfriend(s) have no awareness that they may be feeling *trapped* because they **are captured**, and it's not the woman who is doing it; it's the devil. Many times, but not always the women they meet that they are wary of may be a woman that God has either sent or has allowed to come into a man's life to bring a brother a

Word of deliverance. This one said early on, *"Why do I keep meeting all these nice-looking women who are into God?"*

I responded, *"Because God loves you and He is trying to save your soul."*

Like a hot air balloon, those pretty words floated right over his head. His handsome little head that is filled with images of club dancers, strippers, porn actresses and exciting, illicit sex – the same stuff that got him into this spirit spouse mess, or if it was generational/ancestral, it's the stuff that has kept him in this mess.

And that strip club set is what he is most interested via the spirit of lust and he may think those women are easier, after all they are transactional. Spirit spouse will allow those types sooner than a godly woman because spirit spouse doesn't want to get cast out and spirit spouse is only threatened by a woman that Boyfriend may be serious about and may want to marry.

Regarding spirit spouse he's not spiritually savvy enough to know that she (or they) have him on lockdown. He's not teachable enough to learn about it right now.

He's not strong enough spiritually to do anything about it. In his particular case bloodline issues bolt him down even tighter to evil foundation so that he cannot rise. He's brilliant, handsome, but he's both captured and locked down.

Don't get me wrong, I'm not bitter. I'm not telling this story because he chose spirit spouse and not me. The man doesn't even know that he chose spirit spouse because he doesn't believe spirit spouse exists. He also doesn't know that he didn't choose me because like so many men, he thinks the breadcrumbs will keep me coming to his house like Hansel and Gretel looking for a gingerbread house in the forest. Nope. I don't need any breadcrumbs; I am not making stuffing right now.

He also didn't really choose spirit spouse; he chose money. From what I know about him so far, he may always choose money.

Boyfriend believes in the conglomeration, the amalgamation of all "religions" *a-la-Oprah*. In Oprah's quest to try to make people see that they were more alike than they were different, she allowed many guests on her platform to talk about all their various kinds of kinder, gentler religions. Everyone clapped and got a car, so it must be true. It's not. Don't get me wrong, I love Oprah, but there are many religions and some folks rolled them all into one convenient burrito because they saw all these guests on her famous talk show.

Boyfriend believes that even though he's a man now, he thinks he will come back again, reincarnated as something else--, which is NOWHERE in the Bible. He's thinking he may become something else, like a tree or a butterfly. I guess he hasn't taken the time, or he doesn't have the Bible knowledge to know that **man** is created a little lower than Elohim, in the image and likeness of God, a little lower than the angels, they say. He hasn't realized that coming back as an animal, an insect or a tree is a serious **demotion**.

As we prosper our souls, we get **promoted**, not *demoted*. We do not get promoted to being different beings, but while we live this one Earth life, we prosper in our health and in our money **as** our souls prosper.

We all need to think, sometimes. If prosperity of health and wealth is diminishing, perhaps we should look in the spiritual to see WHY.

A person should be free to choose whatever and whomever they will, spiritually speaking but my sadness is mostly because Boyfriend hasn't fully chosen and embraced God. No one can get to the Father except by Jesus. Jesus is the Way, the Truth and the Life. Boyfriend's only way out of these spiritual and soulish prisons and captivity is by Jesus Christ.

That is why I've written this book for those who want to learn **without having to suffer** and **for those who have suffered** or **who are suffering to find a way out of suffering and prosper their souls**.

Soul Prosperity

Soul prosperity equals being so free in the Lord that you have ZERO *spirit spouses*. Spirit spouses can lead to barrenness in men and women. See how your health is affected by spiritual matters. See how spiritual matters can suffer when the SOUL is running a man's or a woman's life? See how this all started with the memory that wasn't handled God's way and became a soul tie. The soul-tie, or extreme desire – maybe there never was a real person connected to the desire, but it became a *fantasy* that conjured up a whole demon which gladly disguised itself over and again, as *whomever* in your dream or night life and created a whole spiritual nightmare for you.

Now you need deliverance, big time.

A person can have more than one spirit spouse. Also, based on your destiny in God there may be many spirit spouses attached to you to try to derail you, take you down and keep you from reaching destiny. The more important you are to God, the greater your attacks will be.

If you're not important to God or if you are already serving the devil most likely your attacks will be few or none.

Health Issues

In the here and now spirit spouse affects your health. It affects your sleep. Sleep deprivation, worry, stress are contributors to health problems. People who have these encounters end up with mystery diseases, some are mystery symptoms that make no sense and no one knows what is wrong with the victim. *Oh, here comes that crazy woman again, wonder what's wrong with her now,* the doctor or the nurse might say. They run test after test, and there is nothing wrong with you.

Medical bills, prescription bills, office visit copays. Feminine hygiene products, OTC yeast cures. Frustration. Pain. Time constantly researching, *What's wrong with me?* The emotional stigma.

Later on infertility treatments, meds, IVF which is very expensive.

Missed days from work, divided dedication to career and marriage because of reproductive or conception issues.

Emotional upheaval. All from a spiritual source that I'm telling you about. Don't wait to find out on your own. Be teachable, let people tell you things and teach you things to save precious time so you will have a prosperous and healthy, all-sufficient life.

That's what teachers are for to help you not have to learn it on your own. Think about it, you could learn something *else* on your own and take your knowledge, wisdom and understanding to a whole new level and not have to figure out what your grandparents and parents have already had to painfully figure out all over again. When that's the case your family is not prospering, church or no church, if you and the next generations are not learning, but instead making the same mistakes all over again, they are only treading water.

Money Issues

Spirit spouse siphons your money. How? Medical bills. Over-the-counter cures for things that you want to "fix" before anyone finds out, or medical insurance copays, or things that you think will make it go away.

One of the worst things you can do to try to fix this is to seek a fortune teller, tarot reader, witch, wizard, diviner, astrologer, herbalist, evil priest, any one who dabbles in the black ars. To help you get rid of it. More money. And more problems. The trick is with these types they are not thinking of you or trying to help you at all, they are there to help *themselves*. Help themselves get paid, yes and whatever they can get from some unsuspecting dupe who may come to them.

Gifts from Witches

Oh did I mention that a witch can actually **send you a spirit spouse**. If you're not a sinner and there were no sinners in your bloodline it won't stick because no curse can alight without a cause. But who has not sinned and fallen short of the Glory of God? Okay, none of us.

So if you have sinned, have you repented? Have you repented down your bloodline? Then if you are walking in Godly protection, keeping your mind stayed on Jesus, with a prospered soul, then that curse will never alight into your life; it will not stick.

However, if there is sin your bloodline, especially witchcraft, idolatry, or divination you will be *subject to* witchcraft. Your parents could have dedicated you as a baby or young child. You could already be a witch and not know it. Adult witches have baby witches. Are your parents witches/warlocks? By "dedication," your parents could have already married you off in the spirit to someone that they think would bring them success, wealth, fame, an easy life, or they could have been duped into thinking they were assuring your future by marrying you off to some spiritual entity. What they may have ignorantly done is marry you in the spirit and as soon as they did that you were *assigned* a spirit spouse. When this spirit spouse would have come to you, I can't say, but if it happened to you, you know. You could most likely tell me unless it has been wiped from your dream or other memory or if it is a hidden spirit spouse.

God gives us memory because He has nothing to hide. The devil will either give an evil memory, or wipe memory because he has everything to hide.

Your Friends Should Not be Witches

Birds of a feather, they say, flock together. Your friends should not be witches. Your friends should not be blind witches either. Two can't walk together unless they agree.

Don't say you don't know--, don't say you've never met a person that you may think is your friend and you have confided in them, then either sooner or later, maybe too much later you may learn that every time you start talking about anything or any problem you have that "friend" (fake friend) seems to be listening, but they are **not** hearing you. They hear your voice, but they are not hearing your heart or your woes. They don't listen with a compassionate ear, they don't have compassion, at least not for you. They are listening to hear **what is in it for THEM**, as you are flailing, suffering and feel that you are falling or sinking.

There. You feel better now, you've vented. NO! You just let an evil human agent know the blueprint for how they can rip you off or try to rip you off.

No, I'm not jaded or cynical – I've just lived a while. Some of these people, many of these people are in YOUR own family. Maybe your closest confidante.

A brother is born for adversity.

(Proverbs 17:17)

Have you not ever noticed that most people you go to for help – let's say financial help require you to tell them ALL of your financial business and there you are with bated breath hoping, secretly praying and expecting them to save the day? It not like you're asking for a gift, usually you are asking for a short term loan. But then they turn you down. This could be a well-off friend or family member.

You are pouring your heart out, putting all your business out there, but they turn you down, they don't offer any "help" because THERE IS NOTHING IN IT FOR THEM. When they don't even NEED anything--, you do. When there IS NOTHING IN IT FOR THEM, then they are usually not interested.

I'm not lying. I've seen it over and over.

A woman confided in her older brother, who was known for being financially stable. She wasn't trying to get money or help from him; she was trying to get counsel regarding a broken marriage and the behavior of her estranged husband. After she concluded telling her WHOLE story because that was required of her by her brother… what he next said shocked her. His comments included no help to her.

The sister had broken up with her husband and then later found that her late model car, which she *owned* outright **before** they got married had somehow been "refinanced" and now that she was broken up with the husband after a short marriage and she was no longer working a job. The divorce papers were all signed, all the financial settlements had been ratified, she found out that her ex had used the car in some type of loan so now a monthly note was now due again on the car that she *used to own outright.* This "refinance" he did involving the car was a cash for car title type deal. But how had he done it with the car only in her name?

Criminal.

Coming out of the marriage and having to re-establish living arrangements, and et cetera, she didn't have enough money for this extra payment, nor should she have had to pay as this was not disclosed in the divorce agreement. It wasn't that the car was about to be repossessed by the bank or anything that dire, she wanted counsel from her brother on the mind of men and what she could do about this to remedy the situation.

The woman's brother however, said, *"How much do you owe on the car?"*

She told him.

He said to her, *"I'll buy the car from you for the amount that is now owing on it."*

She said, *"Then I won't have a car, and why would I sell it to you for a fraction of what it is worth?"*

That's all he had to say. That's all they had to say to one another. They haven't spoken since that day because she realized when she was pouring out her heart and pouring out her life, her own brother wasn't hearing **her**, he was only filtering out what was in it for him.

That's the surest sign that you've been talking to a person who is **prospered in their flesh**, not their *souls*. Pray you are not one of those people.

She felt as though she had been duped by **two** men, one she understood being an antagonistic ex, but her own brother!

A friend loveth at all times, And a brother is born for adversity. Proverbs 17:17

She did not sell the car to him, which would have really been *giving* the car to him. God supplied a job that paid enough to pay off the car by making the high interest payments which were in the Ex-husband's name but attached by a lien to *her* car. The Ex kept the money that he had unscrupulously borrowed against her car, while he had a car of his own which he had not hocked for cash. (one of those car title loans).

The Lord will repay, and vengeance is God's.

As for her, that was a perfect time to fly off the handle. Even if she hadn't with the Ex because of his rip off she could have connected those two events together and it could have gotten bad, but it didn't. Our sister seems to have soul prosperity even while neither of the two men did.

A prospered soul does not try to rip others off.

Keep Your Business

To Yourself

Girlfriends: Don't tell all your private relationship stories to people who you do not **_absolutely know_** are your friends. Next thing you know that former "friend" will be married to _your_ husband. Your husband was a really a good guy and you loved him, you were just mad at him a couple of times and happened to vent to your fake girlfriend. This gave her a foothold to have something to talk to him about… and she _finessed_ him leaving you and marrying him. Come on, you told her exactly what you two were fighting about and his stance on the issue. All she had to do is agree with him, quietly secretly and become his confidante, much like she used to be yours.

Unprospered souls do not make good friends, or any kind of friend. They are always self-seeking and self-serving. Pray that isn't you.

Had your soul been prospered, you never would have talked down your covenant husband to anyone, unless you *really* wanted to break up. Divorce hits your money because ***divorce is division***. God said, **"Be fruitful and multiply."** God did not say *divide*.

The *spirit of division* is from the devil and of the devil. Divorces cost a lot, emotionally, financially and sometimes physically, as well. Unless you are getting divorced from the worst ogre in the world, divorce is not a soul prospering experience.

Divorce affects the prosperity of the children involved, physically and spiritually as well as their soul prosperity. Many times children think the absent spouse divorced *them*. Many times they think it's their fault. They take on or are given unhealthy emotional burdens that kids shouldn't have to carry and really can't sponsor—especially if one or both of their parents do not have prospered souls and they are downloading on the kids or try to make children their "best friends" instead of their *kids*. Divorce affects them later in their lives in their relationships.

Divorce can often be the effort of a spirit spouse, from any place, but you can see the fruit of your actions when you are the one who conjured up a fantasy spirit spouse. I pray this book has helped you to see that and to repent and change your ways so that you don't cultivate that into our life, into your marriage or into your children's lives or your family's bloodline.

*See the Warfare Prayer Channel on Youtube for prayers against many of the issues discussed in this book:

https://www.youtube.com/channel/UCrgZF7z-fTjgy_ou8IPg4xQ

Dear Reader

Thank you for acquiring, reading, and sharing this book. I pray that it will make you wiser and better equipped to deal with what may come up against you. Better than that, may you preempt the strikes the enemy has planned against you by being *prayed up.*

God bless you,

In the Name of Jesus,

Amen.

Dr. Marlene Miles

Prayer books by this author

While most books by this author have prayer points either throughout the book or at the end, there are some books that are **only** prayers. You just open up the book and pray. They are listed below:

Prayers Against Barrenness: *For Success in Business and Life*

Fruit of the Womb: *Prayers Against Barrenness*

Beauty Curses, *Warfare Prayers Against*
https://a.co/d/5Xlc20M

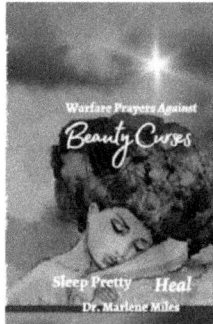

Courts of Marriage: Prayers for Marriage in the Courts of Heaven *(prayerbook)*
https://a.co/d/cNAdgAq

Courtroom Warfare @ Midnight *(prayerbook)*
https://a.co/d/5fc7Qdp

Demonic Cobwebs *(prayerbook)* https://a.co/d/fp9Oa2H

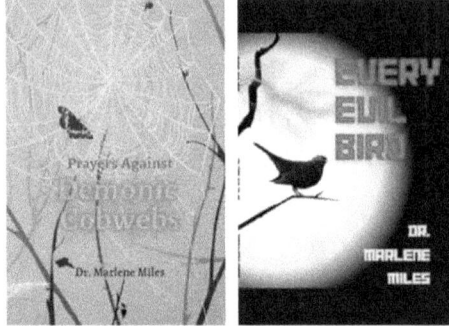

Every Evil Bird https://a.co/d/hF1kh1O

Every Evil Arrow https://a.co/d/afgRkiA

Gates of Thanksgiving

Spirits of Death & the Grave, Pass Over Me and My House https://a.co/d/dS4ewyr

*Please note that my name is spelled incorrectly on amazon, but not on the book.

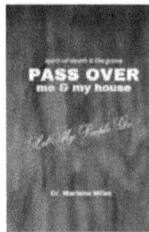

Throne of Grace: Courtroom Prayer

https://a.co/d/fNMxcM9

Warfare Prayer Against Poverty
https://a.co/d/bZ61lYu

Other books by this author

Abundance of Jesus, *The*

AK: *The Adventures of the Agape Kid*

AMONG SOME THIEVES

Ancestral Powers https://a.co/d/9prTyFf

Backstabbers https://a.co/d/gi8iBxf

Barrenness, *Prayers Against*
https://a.co/d/feUltIs

Battlefield of Marriage, *The*

Beware of the Dog: *Prayers Against Dogs in the Dream*

Blindsided: *Has the Old Man Bewitched You?*
https://a.co/d/5O2fLLR

Break Free from Collective Captivity

Caged Life https://a.co/d/0eKxbU9H

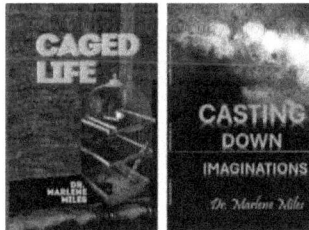

Casting Down Imaginations
https://a.co/d/1UxlLqa

Churchcraft: Witchcraft In the Church

Churchzilla, The Wanna-Be, Supposed-to-be Bride of Christ

Curses of Blind Men

Demonic Cobwebs (prayerbook)

Demonic Time Bombs

Demons Hate Questions (mini book)

Devil Loves Trauma, *The*

Devil Weapons: Unforgiveness, Bitterness,…

The Devourers: *Thieves of Darkness 2*

Do Not Swear by the Moon

Don't Refuse Me, Lord (4 book series)
https://a.co/d/idP34LG

Dream Defilement

The Emptiers: *Thieves of Darkness, 1*
https://a.co/d/5I4n5mc

Every Evil Arrow https://a.co/d/afgRkiA

Evil Touch https://a.co/d/gSGGpS1

Failed Assignment https://a.co/d/3CXtjZY

Fantasy Spirit Spouse https://a.co/d/hW7oYbX

FAT Demons (The): *Breaking Demonic Curses*

The Fold (5-book series)

- The Fold (Book 1)
- Name Your Seed (Book 2)
- The Poor Attitudes of Money (3)
- Do Not Orphan Your Seed (4)
- For the Sake of the Gospel (5)
- My Sowing Journal

Gang Ups: *Touch Not God's Anointed*

got HEALING? Verses for Life

got LOVE? Verses for Life

got HOPE? Verses for Life

got money? https://a.co/d/g2av41N

Has My Soul Been Sold?

How to Dental Assist

How to Dental Assist2: Be Productive, Not Wasteful

I Take It Back

Legacy

Let Me Have A Dollar's Worth
https://a.co/d/h8F8XgE

Level the Playing Field
https://www.youtube.com/watch?v=BfF-TX1EWNQ

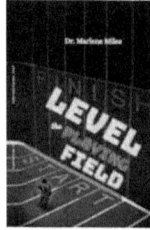

Living for the NOW of God

Lose My Location https://a.co/d/crD6mV9

Love Breaks Your Heart

Man Safari, *The* (mini book from The Wilderness Romance)

Marriage Ed. Rules of Engagement & Marriage

Made Perfect in Love

Money Hunters: Beware of Those

Money on the Altar https://a.co/d/4EqJ2Nr

Mulberry Tree https://a.co/d/9nR9rRb

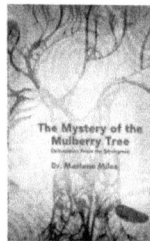

Motherboard (The) - *Soul Prosperity Series*

Name Your Seed

Occupy: *Until I Return*

Plantation Souls

Players Gonna Play

Power Money: Nine Times the Tithe
https://a.co/d/gRt41gy

Powers Above

Repent of Visiting Evil Altars
https://a.co/d/3n3Zjwx

The Robe, *Part 1, The Lessons of Joseph*

The Robe, *The Lessons of Joseph* Part II,

Seasons of Grief

Seasons of Waiting

Seasons of War

Second Marriage, Third--, *Any Marriage*

https://a.co/d/6m6GN4N

Sift You Like Wheat

Six Men Short: What Has Happened to all the Men?

Son https://a.co/d/09mIThSg

Soul Prosperity, Soul Prosperity Series Bk 3
https://a.co/d/5p8YvCN

Souls Captivity, Soul Prosperity Series Book 2

The Spirit of Poverty

StarStruck

SUNBLOCK

The Swallowers: *Thieves of Darkness*, Book 3

Take It Back

This Is NOT That: How to Keep Demons from Coming at You

Time Is of the Essence

Too Many Wives: *Why You Have Lady Problems*

Tormenting Spirits   https://a.co/d/dAogEJf

Toxic Souls

Triangular Power *(series)*

- Powers Above
- SUNBLOCK
- Do Not Swear by the Moon
- STARSTRUCK

Unbreak My Heart: *Don't Let Me Die*
Uncontested Doom

Unguarded Hours, *The*

Unseen Life, *The* https://a.co/d/0drZ5Ll

Upgrade: How to Get Out of Survival Mode (and two more titles):

- Toxic Souls (Book 2 of series)
- Legacy (Book 3 of series)

WTH? Get Me Out of This Hell

The Wasters: *Thieves of Darkness,* Bk 2
https://a.co/d/bUvI9Jo

What Have You to Declare? What Do You Have With You from Where You've Been?

When I Was A Child, *I Prayed As a Child*

When the Devourer is Rebuked

https://a.co/d/1HVv8oq

The Wilderness Romance *(series)* This series is about conducting a Godly relationship and marriage with someone who is a Wilderness person. It is about how to recognize it and navigate through it. These books are about how not to get caught up in such.

- *The Social Wilderness*
- *The Sexual Wilderness*
- *The Spiritual Wilderness*

Other Series

Matters of the Heart series

Made Perfect in Love https://a.co/d/70MQW3O

Love Breaks Your Heart https://a.co/d/4KvuQLZ

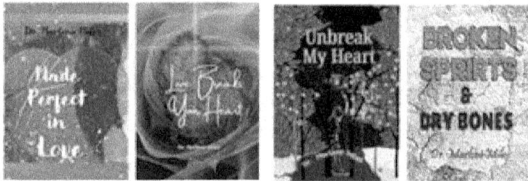

Unbreak My Heart https://a.co/d/84ceZ6M

Broken Spirits & Dry Bones https://a.co/d/e6iedNP

The Fold (a series on Godly finances)

https://a.co/d/4hz3unj

Soul Prosperity Series https://a.co/d/bz2M42q

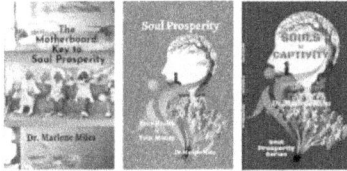

Spirit Spouse books

https://a.co/d/9VehDSo

https://a.co/d/97sKOwm

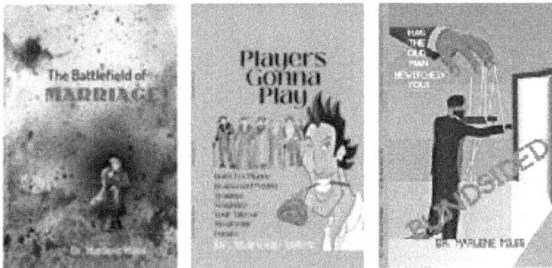

Thieves of Darkness series

https://a.co/d/b07c8Ms

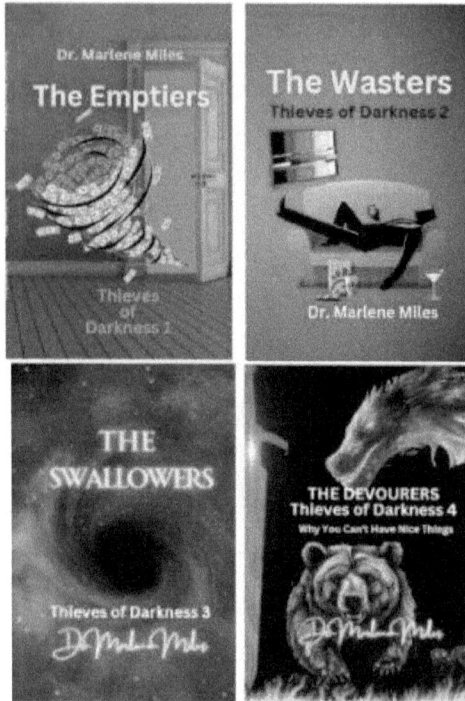

Triangular Powers https://a.co/d/aUCjAWC

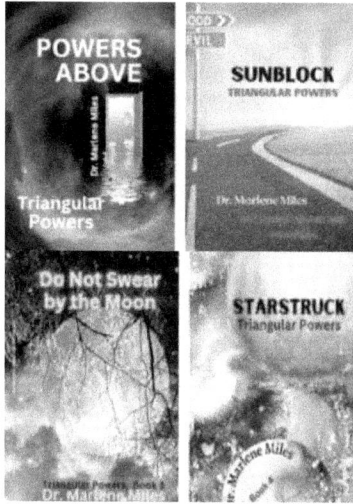

Upgrade (series) *How to Get Out of Survival Mode*
https://a.co/d/aTERhXO